How To Be A Good Preacher

Being a Workman That's Not Ashamed

Published by Dwayne and Cheryl Shigg

This book was previously published under the name Preacher 101

Dedication

To all of the preachers that will preach the word in season and out.

To all of the "God talkers" that have invested in me.

TABLE OF CONTENTS

Foreword

I believe Dr. Dwayne E. Shigg has captured the heart of the apostle Paul as it relates to edifying but also correcting the modern day Timothy. In this current age where there is a great lack of fathering (spiritually) and son accountability, Dr. Shigg brings a fresh voice to a long needed reawakening of this Biblical principle.

In this insightful reading: preachers can be enlightened on various subjects that pertain to ministry from education to etiquette, preaching to personhood, holiness to humility, giftedness to graciousness, assignment to assessment, calling to commitment, and from preparedness to presentation...

How to Be A Good Preacher is a must-read for the beginner preacher and the experienced alike. This book should be a required reading for those seeking licensing or ordination. How to Be a Good Preacher has a universal denominational structure with a nondenominational appeal.

What comes to light in this book by Dr. Shigg is the culmination of over three decades of ministry, commitment, and academia. How to Be A Good Preacher is a spiritually insightful book while still practical and simplistic.

Like a phrase I've coined, "From GED to PHD," this book is an easy read with golden nuggets of revelation for preachers at all stations of maturity.

Bishop W. Todd Ervin Sr., MTh.

Church One Ministries, Long Beach California

Introduction

My name is Dwayne E Shigg, I have been preaching for over thirty years. I have been a pastor of two churches, over a 17 year period. Holy Bible Way Church in Long Beach in Compton, Ca. and the Christ Fellowship Church in West Covina, Ca. I have had the blessing of being taught by some of the greatest men of God.

In my travels I have seen preachers display behavior that demonstrated that they had no, as the saying goes, home training. Such behavior that may cause some people to say "don't they know better than that" I guess the answer would be, no they don't. That is one of the reasons that make this book a burden and a necessity.

Some of the things that I have seen people do provoke some questions and critiques but I have to remember something that my wife has often said to me, which is that everyone has not had the training that I have had? Now before you stop reading and start thinking that I have an inflated ego, I do not think I know everything. I have had my share of mess ups and doing dumb things. Which is another reason for this book. To keep you from making some of the same mistakes that I have made and also to add to other good training information that many have already brought forth. It is just painful to see some of the things that pass for preaching, especially with all of the helps that are available today.

For some people, the ideas in this book will not be new but just a review, for others they will be fresh information. The purpose of this writing is two-fold. It will give the new preacher information that will help them in their ministry. By new I mean those that are dealing with a call, recently began preaching and those that have been preaching for a short while, 7 years or so. But the information can be helpful or a refresher course for those that may have been preaching for a little longer.

This book is also a tool to help Pastors with those preachers that are under their leadership. It can be a help or mentoring tool in the spirit of a Moses to Joshua or Paul to Timothy, or a Manuel Scott Sr. to Dwayne Shigg.

I trust that there is benefit for all who read these pages. May you find words that will help you to be an effective preacher. I trust that you will be challenged to think, to change and to be the best proclaimer of the gospel that you are meant to be.

And going on from thence, he saw other two brethren, James the son of Zebedee, and John his brother, in a ship with Zebedee their father, mending their nets; and he called them. And they immediately left the ship and their father, and followed him-Mth 4:21-22

Know That You Are Called

It is most important that you KNOW that you are called by God. Preaching is not a game. Not a career that YOU decide that you want to go into. To describe it, I would use a term that we hear in the wedding vows, not to be entered into lightly or unadvisedly. Why should a person go in the preaching ministry one may ask? This may sound like an elementary question to ask. You may be surprised to hear some of the REAL reasons that people go into the preaching ministry.

My nephew Lester once asked me why did I become a preacher? The answer that I gave him could be thought of as a cliché' but my answer was, "that's what the Lord told me to do". Preachers need to know and make sure that they were "called" by God. There are so many reasons that some people begin preaching and some of them have nothing to do with the Lord's direction.

Some people come into this because they think it is glamorous, some people want a lot of attention. Some are on a power trip, some people start preaching with good intentions but they can still be the wrong reasons. Intentions such as, you want to see people saved-that's good! You want to spread the gospel – that's good. You want to serve the Lord. Those are all real good intentions but those are things that should concern ALL believer no matter what area one may work in. Those things don't automatically translate into going in to the preaching ministry in a formal sense.

Sometimes people can be guided by the wrong people and the wrong motivations. Perhaps your grandfather was a preacher (as was mine) or your father was a preacher. Maybe some elderly saint in the church may have said to you "you are going to preach someday". Somebody has said to you or about you, "that's a preacher right there". All or some of these may have happened to you, you may be contemplating them but DON'T MAKE A DECISIONTO PREACH

BASED ON THEM. That decision is really not yours to make, it's the Lords.

The bible says in 1 Tim 1:11-12:

> *According to the glorious gospel of the blessed God, which was committed to my trust. And I thank Christ Jesus our Lord, who hath enabled me, for that he counted me faithful, putting me into the ministry;*

Paul thanks the Lord for *putting* him into ministry. The word putting in that text is translated from a Greek word *"tithemi"*, which means to place or to set. This shows that it was not Paul's idea to go into the preaching ministry. It was the Lord's doing, Paul accepted and obeyed his placement, his setting into the ministry.

In the account in the book of Matthew when Jesus called the fisherman in 4:21:

> *And going on from thence, he saw other two brethren, James the son of Zebedee, and John his brother, in a ship with Zebedee their father, mending their nets; and he called them.*

The word called in that text is the word *kaleō (kal-eh'-o)* which means to bid, call (forth). Jesus initiated the idea or transaction for them to come into the preaching ministry or to become fishers of men.

In the book of Exodus 3:3-4 the bible records:

*And Moses said, I will now turn aside, and see
this great sight, why the bush is not burnt. And
when the Lord saw that he turned aside to see,
God called unto him out of the midst of the
bush, and said, Moses, Moses. And he said,
here am I.*

The word *called* in verse 4 is the word qârâ'-
(*kaw-raw'*) - which is defined as having the idea of
accosting a person met, to *call* out to. When you think
of accosting, the idea is aggressive or forceful. In other
words a calling is not a nice request; it can
be more like a BENEVOLENT CONVINCING or
PURSUASION.

The preaching ministry is not what I had
planned for my life. I went to school for broadcasting.
I wanted to play music on the radio and do voiceovers
for commercials. BUT the Lord had other plans for my
life's work regarding the direction and purpose for my
life. That does not mean that I can't be on the radio,
as a matter of fact I have been on three different
radio stations in Southern California. But that is not
the MAIN focus of my life.

The Lord called and I answered. I am in the
preaching ministry not because my mother is a
preacher, not because my grandfather was a

preacher, not because my great grandfather was a preacher, not because my uncle is a preacher, but because that's what the Lord said for Dwayne Emanuel Shigg to do.

Don't let anyone push you into preaching. They will not be there when you need some inspiration for what to preach and they don't have any anointing for you to preach it. They won't be there through the rough times and attacks and they don't have the right weapons to defeat those attacks.

Once YOU KNOW that you are supposed to preach, after you have prayed, fasted, whatever your spiritual process is for clarification, talked to your Pastor,(you should not just hear a voice or SOMETHING TELLING YOU and jump right into this thing), don't let people's opinion keep you from obeying God. You may hear comments like: you don't know enough, I don't think you have been saved long enough. You are from the wrong background (whatever that means). Many of the people that God called in the bible had some strikes on their record. You may also hear that you don't have that preacher look or nobody else in your family is a preacher. Once you KNOW what you are to do, OBEY GOD.

Please, please, please, if you are not supposed to be preaching, don't do it. Witness, usher, sing, work with the audio in the church, find out what your calling is but if HE didn't call you to preach, DON'T DO IT.

You may ask the question, how will you know? The answer is, if God really called you, you will know. Once you do know and you have accepted and obeyed the Lord do not keep trying to PROVE to people that you have been called and that you are a preacher, just preach the word !!!

Women Preachers

The above information is good for all that are in the preaching ministry but I would like to take a little time to speak with the ladies that say they have been called to preach. I am not even going to deal with is it right or is it wrong, does God really call women to preach? Whatever you believe, you deal with God on that.

LADIES,SISTERS, if you say that you have been called, you have prayed, fasted, talked to your Husband (if that applies), your Pastor and you KNOW that God called you to preach based on sound biblical reasoning and Godly direction and you KNOW that you are not violating any biblical principles, that's what you have to do, PREACH THE WORD.

You are preaching because that's what He said

to do. You are not trying to PROVE something to anybody, you are not preaching because God couldn't find enough men or the right man. Not because you think men have not done a good job. If you are preaching, ladies make SURE that is what GOD told you to do.

Don't waste time trying to justify your preaching, trying to prove to anyone that you are a legitimate preacher or that you are as good as "any man". If you are called to preach, DO THAT. Some will accept it and some will not. Don't try to convince anyone or get approval, it is a waste of time. PREACH the word; you want GOD to say well done MY good and faithful servant.

To reiterate, for all that are preaching, make sure that you are CALLED BY GOD!

But Jesus called them to him, and saith unto them, Ye know that they which are accounted to rule over the Gentiles exercise lordship over them; and their great ones exercise authority upon them. But so shall it not be among you: but whosoever will be great among you shall be your minister- (Servant) Mark 10:42-43

Having a Servant's Attitude

I think it is important to talk about servant hood but in addition to that, another word is important and that is PATIENCE. It is important that those coming into the preaching ministry and those that are already there, have patience. Too many people today are getting saved on Sunday, preaching on Tuesday, they want to Pastor by Friday and they are a Bishop the following week. You need to take some time, go sit down somewhere and LEARN something. Paul's story of coming to know Jesus is told in Acts 9. The beginning of his "preaching ministry" starts in verse 20, but in verse

19 the bible says that he spent time with the disciples. Jesus called his disciples in Matthew 4, He spent time preparing them (chapters 5-9) before he sent them out (chapter 10). Don't be in too much of a hurry, your turn and time will come but will you be prepared when it does? Learn how to wait and learn how to be a waiter while you are waiting.

It is extremely important to have a servant's attitude. Because that's what we are, the Lord's servants. The Bible tells us that the way to demonstrate greatness is by serving. Often when people get called to the preaching ministry, they may have some crazy ideas that this places them on some kind of pedestal or they think that people are supposed to serve them, WRONG. Be careful of that kind of thinking. Accepting the call to preach is accepting a call to SERVICE. Along with that call, comes baggage. People are not always going to like or agree with what you are saying, especially when it is the TRUTH about them. Through all of the ups and downs, people saying this and saying that, preachers are to serve God. We can do that by serving others in the capacity that He calls us to.

In Mark 10 the scripture shows the Lord speaking to the disciples about greatness and He says, to be great you have to be a minister. The word in that text does not mean "preacher". It is the word diakonos (*dee-ak'-on-os)* which means: to *run* on errands; an *attendant*, that is, (generally) a *waiter* (at table or in other menial duties).

When a person is a "waiter" they don't decide what they serve, the person that they are waiting on does. This is the idea of being a "waiter". There may be times when waiters don't decide what section of the restaurant they will work in.

I don't know about you but when I go to a restaurant and I may need something extra, a straw or napkins, I may not wait for "my" waiter or waitress I may ask whoever is dressed in the uniform of those working in that place and If they are good *diakrinos'*, they will either get it or inform someone that I need it. In other words, if preachers are going to be good ministers, servants, it may require serving in some areas that is not "your" station, not what is "your" preference, at least for a little while, why? Because that is what is needed at the time. You may be the preacher over the youth but you may be needed to work the audio, you may be needed to work with the children, serve communion to someone, help move a chair or something. Why should you do that?, that's not "preaching", no but it is "serving" and that's what you are, a SERVANT.

Another important thing about serving and preaching is that preaching may not involve the idea of rights but it does have a lot to do with responsibility. Just like the waiter has certain responsibilities: writing down the order, having a good attitude, getting you extra straws, napkins or whatever you need. There are some things that preachers are responsible for. Being ready and prepared to preach or serve when the need or opportunity arrives. There is a responsibility to be available for service. There is a responsibility to grow, to take care of yourself so that you will be available and prepared when the opportunity comes.

Another thing to remember is to be a help to your Pastor in whatever way that you can, we will also talk more about this later. Not only do you obviously want to be helpful to the Pastor but to visiting ministers. Service to them may be shown in several ways. From getting a glass of water, to hanging up a coat, to parking a car. Too many times preachers let their egos get in the way and they don't take on a servant's heart and attitude. I did not say slave or flunky but servant. Making things easier for the Pastor or visiting preacher can result in good things for you. You can get a chance to grow; you will reap what you have sown. Your motivation for serving should be to help, not kissing up. Having a servant's attitude will be to your benefit in the long run.

An interesting thing about servants is that they may serve in more than one place or temporarily serve in a particular place because that is where the need is. Those in the preaching ministry are called preachers but they are also called ministers, which, as I said earlier, means servant. I sometimes want to ask the question, are you a minister or "just" a preacher? What do I mean by that? There are other ways of serving besides preaching in front of the congregation on Sunday morning. In fact if you are rather new to the preaching ministry, you will not be preaching in front of the congregation any time soon or with any regularity. Preaching in front of a congregation on a Sunday morning is not the ONLY place for a preacher to serve. There is bible study, Sunday school, serving at the altar when people come to give their life to Christ or join the church.

At a church where a friend of mine is Pastor, the alter workers are preachers. They go to the back and work with the people, finding out what the need is. It may include: salvation, prayer or new membership, they are "ministering" but they are not "preaching" and it is likely that those that serve in those places are likely to be given an opportunity to "preach" before those that are just waiting for a preaching turn.

There are other places to preach or teach besides the church house. There are convalescent homes, transitional living houses, places where people are incarcerated, to name a few but make sure that these are places that you believe you are called to go to, each of them have different dynamics and the people may have different needs.

This is why it is important for you to take your time. Your "turn" will come but the question is what are you doing now? I remember reading "somewhere" that if you will be faithful over a few things, you will be made ruler over many. Are you preparing yourself and growing where you are so that you will be ready when the opportunity DOES come.

I want to say a word about PASTORING. All of you are not going to serve as a Senior Pastor of a congregation. All of you are not meant to be. You will not all be a Moses, there is a need for some Joshuas, and there are some Pauls that need a Silas or Timothy. There will be someone that is meant to be the senior Pastor but there will be a need for an assistant, for a youth pastor, Christian Education Pastor, men's ministry "Pastor", women's ministry "Pastor" (in some churches the person over the particular ministry is called a director and in some they are called the Pastor. That is why it is important to know what you are called to do. Wait your turn; work where you are and what you are supposed to be will come to light.

And Samuel said, Hath the Lord as great delight in burnt offerings and sacrifices, as in obeying the voice of the Lord? Behold, to obey is better than sacrifice, and to hearken than the fat of rams. 1 Samuel 15:22

Follow Directions

I want to look at the principle of following directions as it relates to three different areas, the first one is:

Task

Sometimes while participating in the worship services, you may be asked to pray, read a scripture or do something else in the meeting. It is important that you honor the request. However, sometimes when a preacher has not been used often or is new in the ministry or maybe they think more of themselves than they should, there can be a temptation to use these situations as an opportunity to show off or make a name for yourself, score some points or something like that. WRONG, DO WHAT YOU ARE TOLD TO DO!

You would think that it would not be necessary to say something like this but you would be surprised at the great need that there really is for this to be said. Following directions will do more for your reputation than taking the opportunity to try and score some points. Taking the opportunity to show off may get people talking about you alright, but probably not the kind of talk that you want. One thing that Pastors do appreciate is a preacher that follows directions. You may be saying "I saw Rev. Doctor Bishop what's his name do this or that. You may have but if it is in disobedience, it may have not been to their advantage. It may also be that they are someone that is known in that particular church and has some liberties that you don't have. They may have been around a lot longer than you have and can do some things that you can't.

One of the things that happens when you preach when you were told to pray is that it can make you look desperate. It can give you a bad reputation and yes preachers do talk about other preachers, the next time you go somewhere, they may already know about you before you get there and what they know may not be good. You don't have to be desperate and try to MAKE an opportunity. I continue to keep in mind something that I was told by the late Dr. Manuel Scot Sr. He said, if God called you to preach, He will provide a place for you to preach.

It is important that you understand that one of the things that you should NEVER do is get up behind someone that has already preached and re-preach their sermon or deliver a mini sermon, when you are supposed to be doing something else like invitation, offering, giving remarks or whatever. That would be a defective thing to do. Somebody's salvation could be on the line while you are stroking your ego.

Time

Another way this rule of following directions is often violated is when you are given a time limit for your preaching. You may be speaking with several other preachers for an Easter service or New Year's Eve worship or something like that where each preacher is given 10 minutes for example. Sometimes a person will go over their time or they may say something like "if I had more time I would"... or I wish that I had more time, well the fact is, you don't have more time so the thing to do is to properly use the time that you have rather than wasting time wishing that you had more time. It might not even be a bad idea to prepare for 8 minutes, because you may end up using the other two anyway, you will still be in your time. Even if you give back 2 minutes, that would be okay. If you make it a habit of speaking in the time that you are given, you may likely get an invitation to come back and speak without the ten minute time limit. Following this direction can cause you to look good because inevitably there WILL be somebody that will not stay in the time limit.(They obviously were not as smart as you were to buy this book).

Topic

Sometimes there are opportunities to preach when you are given a certain topic to preach on. I have seen this done for special occasions such as Easter or a worship meeting on New Year's Eve. A preacher is given a word that begins with each letter spelling our Easter or New Year. This is also done in what is called in some cultures, the 7 last sayings of Christ on the cross. Each preacher is given a verse that corresponds to Jesus' time on the cross. This is often done around Easter. Sometimes a person may not stay with the word or verse that was given to them. There are many reasons for this. It could be that their word isn't "exciting" enough in their mind. The word or verse they have may require some research and they may not take the time it takes to do that (lazy preacher). They may have some other sermons that fit another word but not theirs and they want to just kind of cut and paste a word.

This is not what should be done. Stay with the word or topic that you were given. The same anointing that is on the word you want, can be on the word that you were asked to speak on. The same God that gives the anointing for the other sermons, can give that anointing to this one. There are even times when a person will not stay with their word and say the Holy Ghost lead them or changed things. This is the same Holy Ghost that led that Pastor in putting this together and the same Holy Ghost that leads the Pastor that gave you that certain word. This is the same God that inspired the word that said God is not the author of confusion. This is not the God that would LEAD anyone to blatantly disobey the shepherd of the house that you are preaching in. God is a God of order; it is not likely that you were told by him not to preach what you were told to preach.

If you can't get a word for the direction that you were given, maybe you should decline the assignment. God is an orderly God. When given a certain word or topic from the Pastor to speak, DO WHAT YOU ARE TOLD TO DO!!!

The bible says that you reap what you sow. If you are a person that does not follow directions and if you became a Pastor or a leader over a ministry within the church, you may end up with somebody that does not follow your directions.

The bible teaches that to obey is better than sacrifice. The text in 1Samuel 15 speaks about REBLLION being similar to witchcraft. Can you actually be preaching and practicing WITCHCRAFT?. I don't imagine that God blesses witchcraft, DO YOU?

Let all things be done decently and in order. 1 Corinthians 14:40

Preaching Invitations

Here are a few helpful words about preaching engagements. When you get preaching assignments, make sure they come from the Pastor of the church or at least someone officially designated by the Pastor. The way you do that is, whenever possible, talk to the Pastor. Now in most cases this will not be an issue because it will be the Pastor that asks you anyway.

There may be an occasion when you will get asked by someone from the church, let's say the youth director or the director of the men's ministry. Hopefully they have been given the authority to make the request but maybe they have not, when asked by someone other than the Pastor, your response should be, have the Pastor call me or when can I speak to the Pastor or in some way make sure that you communicate with them.

Doing this allows you to give the Pastor the proper respect and you stay clear of any problems. A problem that you can run into by not talking to the Pastor could be that the person that asked you to preach on the special day gets a yes from you and then goes to the Pastor to see if it is ok and someone else is doing the same thing with another preacher. You may be thinking that you have an assignment and you don't. Making sure that you talk to the Pastor may put you in a good position to be asked back.

When getting a preaching assignment you also need to make sure that you talk to YOUR Pastor. They are your spiritual covering; they need to know about things like this. They may have an assignment for you on that same day or they may know something about the place where you are going to preach. Something that may not be good and they can save you from getting mixed up in something or give you some pointers before you go.

There are those that will always do something,

trying to get a preaching assignment, BE CAREFUL. I was taught by the late Dr. Manuel Scott Sr., never to ask anybody to let you preach, and don't get mad if they don't let you. As was already mentioned, he said if God called you to preach, He would provide a place for you to preach. This has served as good advice for me. I have never had a problem being used.(There are other ways of being used as a preacher besides "preaching") I taught Sunday school, I was a Pastor's assistant and I taught the other preachers on the staff at the church that I attended. I have had preaching opportunities in many different places. I have been the Pastor of 2 churches. I am presently the director of Christian Education, I give direction to the M.I.T's (Ministers in Training) and I assist with the marriage ministry in the church where I worship now, as well as speaking at conferences and preaching opportunities at other churches.

If you are worthy of an opportunity, someone will notice and give you one. When you do that one well, they will tell somebody else and you can get another one. This is how you get opportunities, not by asking. If you have to ask somebody to let you preach, the question will come, why you are always "asking"? The thinking would be, if you were any good or worthy of an opportunity, somebody would be asking you.

So don't worry about the opportunities, they will come. The question is, what are you doing now where you are, how well do you take care of the opportunities that you DO get.

His lord said unto him, Well done, good and faithful servant; thou hast been faithful over a few things, I will make thee ruler over many things: enter thou into the joy of thy lord.

So, do well where you are, Whether therefore ye eat, or drink, or whatsoever ye do…,

Whatsoever thy hand findeth to do… you should be able to finish these verses, if you can't, you don't need more opportunities right now.

Whether therefore ye eat, or drink, or whatsoever ye do, do all to the glory of God. 1 Corinthians 10:31

Helpful Hints

This section is composed of a few pointers that may assist you with your journey in ministry.

It is a good idea to invest in your ministry.

Buy some books or computer software every now and then. Many people have no problem spending money dressing up on the outside, buying new clothes or shoes and other things like that. People will spend plenty on their feet but nothing on their walk. Plenty on their head but nothing on their mind. Invest in yourself; go to a conference every now and then. Take a class; go to school if you can. This helps in making you a vessel that is better equipped for the master's use.

Proper attire

Make sure you dress appropriate. This is not as big of a deal in present times as it once was. It is also not a major factor in some churches but it is still good information to have. In most places a suit and tie is normal dress for preachers and in some places it is not (ladies you can make the appropriate application as it relates to dresses, pants and hats). You don't want to go anywhere, (as my mother would say) looking any old kind of way. If you are preaching at a conference where the atmosphere is relaxed and casual, that may not call for "dressing up", be appropriate for that occasion. Also be appropriate for that particular ministry. They may want anybody that preaches there to be dressed in a suit and tie, dresses below your knee and chest covered. If that is what they want and you accept the engagement then you dress the way they feel is appropriate. If it is TOO "traditional" for you, then maybe you should not accept the assignment. You never want your clothes to make you the attraction, neither do you want to be a distraction because of what you may be wearing.

People may be in church, but they are STILL people. Going back to what was said about talking to your Pastor, this is why it is a good idea, they may know the habits of that particular Pastor and congregation.

It is to your benefit to learn how to be quick to hear and slow to speak.

In other words, shut up sometimes and listen. Even though it seems obvious, this is something that really needs to be said. This can be good advice not just for the new preachers but sometimes for the more experienced preacher as well. Sometimes people can have the tendency to get the BIG HEAD, if you don't know what that means, it means being egotistical. (egos can be a major issue with a lot of preachers), yes even possibly YOU. Because you were called to preach and you are the child of Rev. Big Shot or the grandchild of Rev. Bigger Shot or you preached one good sermon, does not mean that you know everything. When people try to tell you something that can help you, it may be a good idea to listen. Does that mean the information is always helpful? No. Does that mean the information is always correct? No. But you may not know that unless you are willing to listen. Please understand, this is a general rule. You can't listen to EVERYBODY.

Everyone that is telling you something may not be trying to help you. You do want to be careful *who* you listen to, but not be so cocky that you will not listen to anybody. I once read that President Lyndon Johnson had a sign on his desk that read "You are not learning anything if your mouth is open".

Be yourself

There are times when a preacher may look at another preacher and try to copy their style or mannerisms. I'm not talking about picking up some good habits from someone. What I'm talking about is trying to look like someone or moving or acting like they do. For example, Michael Jordon use to stick is tongue out when he was going to the basket. Then, on playgrounds all over the country there would be kids sticking out their tongues. I am sure that they found out that sticking their tongues out didn't make the ball go into the basket. It was not Michael Jordon's *tongue* but Michael Jordon's *talent,* that put the ball in the basket.

Find your own style, your own personality, be yourself. When you imitate someone else it can make you look like a copy of that person and not the original that you are. Everybody has a style that is theirs, even the person you may be trying to copy.

There will be some things that a person picks up because they may have come up under a certain preacher but that is a little different. In cases like that, it's not a case of trying to copy them, it's just natural to have some behavior like your parent in the ministry. Even in that situation you have to be yourself. Some people are teaching preachers, some are singing preachers and some are "hooping" preachers and some are animated. As you continue in your ministry, you will develop a style of your own, your own way of doing things that are parts of the way YOU are. That is the best way for styles and habits to form. The person that you are trying to copy may have a particular reason for doing what they do. It may be something that is a part of their background. Those things may not be a part of you and they may not fit you. Whatever style that is developed, you have to do YOU. There is a saying: You have to do your own growing no matter how tall your grandfather was. In other words you will have to be you.

This next one may not be as prevalent with present day preachers but just in case, here it is.

It is better to be asked up.

Sitting in the pulpit when you go to visiting a church or sitting in the section where the preachers are designated to sit in a particular church, (some don't sit in the pulpit but on the front row for example), for some people is a big deal. Just because you are a preacher does not mean that you are "supposed" to sit in the pulpit in every church that you go to. You should not automatically walk to the pulpit when you go to a visiting church. As the saying goes, it is better to be asked up than to be asked down.

Don't read anything cold

This is just something that can help you if you are reading a scripture in the service. At the beginning of worship in many churches there is someone that prays and someone reads a scripture. If you are told that you are to read a scripture, it's a good idea to go over it. There may be some words that you are not familiar with,(especially if it's an old testament scripture). You don't want to read and stumble over words. There may be a time when you are reading from a different version than you normally carry. Reading over the scripture before you read aloud is just a good habit that can help your reading to go a little smoother.

Don't take liberties

Sometimes when you may be speaking at a church that is not your home church, you may not know what they do and don't "allow". For example, you may come from a place where speaking in unknown tongues is okay. (This is not an attempt to speak for or against the practice of tongues.) If you don't know what the policy is, don't just assume that it is okay (as was said earlier, that's why it is a good idea to talk to your Pastor first). Find out what the practices are at the particular church before you do anything that may be a problem. Please don't go with "well if the Spirit leads me"….The spirit of God is orderly. If that is something that is not done at that church, then you should not do it.

The same thing would be true for laying on hands. You may be "lead" to pray for some people, get permission and you need to know if they are okay with laying on hands when you are praying, ask the Pastor. If you are preaching and the Pastor is not there, ask whoever is in charge. Do not say to them is it okay if I …, they may tell you what "they "feel. Ask them "what is the Pastor's policy on laying on hands, speaking in tongues, prophesying, or whatever. The bible says all things are to be done decently and in ORDER and the Pastor is the one responsible for setting that order.

Learn the books of the bible

If anybody should know where to find certain books of the Bible it SHOULD be those proclaiming the words in the Bible. Have you ever seen a situation at church where the speaker will give a text or asked the people to go to that text and the people in the pulpit don't seem to know where the book is? I know we should not be looking, but you know you do sometimes.

Keep your ego in check

This is one area that can hurt a preacher. Sometimes a person can begin to think more of themselves then they should. This can be fueled by the adulation, the fuss people make over you, the cheers and things that happen when you are preaching. One has to remember that all of it is not really about you, it's the anointing.

Proverbs 16:18 says: Pride goes before destruction and an haughty spirit before a fall. The word *pride* in that text is the word *gâ'ôn (gaw-ohn')* , it means arrogance, Excellency, majesty, pomp, swelling. The word *haughty* in the text is the word gôbahh (*gn'-bah),* it means: elation, grandeur, height, high, loftiness. These words have to do with the idea of one being lifted up. The other part of the verse tells us that nothing good comes from this, the results being destruction and a fall. When your ego gets the best of you, you will experience destruction or a fall in some capacity. It may be personal, professional or positional. Do all that you can to keep your ego under control.

Study to shew thyself approved unto God, a workman that needeth not to be ashamed, rightly dividing the word of truth. 2 Timothy 2:15

Rightly Divide The Word

Another important factor that you should be aware of is the need for study. Yes God will give some revelations through the Holy Spirit. Yes you need to have a regular prayer life. But that is IN ADDITION to study, not INSTEAD of it. The Holy Ghost will give revelation but study brings proper information and interpretation. Sometimes preachers may depend too much on prayer and not study because they are lazy. There are not too many things that are more disgusting and dangerous than a lazy preacher.

There is need for study so that we can tell people what thus says the Lord. That is what they should get, what HE said, not what YOU think, as it relates to Bible principles. How much power and anointing is there on what YOU said or your opinion? I may think a lot of my opinion but it does not scare the devil. It does not mean anything to anybody but me and my wife and sometimes it doesn't mean anything to her. I remember hearing Bishop Kenneth Ulmer say that God is not obligated to honor what YOU say His word says or your opinion about what His word says but He will honor what it DOES say.

2 Timothy 2:15 says study to shew thyself approved unto God. He's the one that we want to say well done. Not the preacher clique or church people. We want to show ourselves approved unto God and rightly divide HIS word of truth. How do you know that you are approved of God? The word approved in that text is the word dokimos (*dok'-ee-mos)* and it means *acceptable*. You will likely be accepted if you rightly divide His word and you have been called by Him.

The scripture says that you are a workman that should rightly divide the word of truth. The words rightly divide in that text are translated from the

Greek word, *orthotomeō* (*or-thot-om-eh'-o)* it means, to make a *straight* cut. A surgeon could do some serious damage if they did not make straight cuts. Can you image the danger when spiritual surgeons don't make straight cuts? We are to tell people what God says. There may sometimes be a tendency to just give people some good sounding slogans and clichés. (lazy preacher) These things may not do much to help in rough times. That is not what will cause the enemy to flee. Slogans and clichés will not keep us from being ashamed and those alone may not qualify as rightly dividing the *word* of truth.

Sometimes there may be a tendency to say something like "I'm going to let the Spirit use me". Some people mean by this, they will just say what they feel the Spirit will give them to say. Letting the Spirit use you is something that is done in addition to study, not instead of it. The Spirit of God is not going to saying anything that is not already said in the word of God, as far as principles are concerned.

I can remember a time when I did, what I called letting the Spirit use me. I did not spend the proper time studying; I was just going to let the Spirit "use" me. This was at the church where I started preaching in Los Angeles and it was in the early

stages of my preaching ministry. Early stages–
translation: when I was young and stupid. This was
one of the worst days of my life. I fell flat on my, uh
let's say "face". I messed up BIG time. The people did
not really get a word that day and to some degree
the enemy got a victory . You can believe that it
NEVER happened again. I made sure that the Lord
directed me on the subject that I was to preach and
I studied the text so I could rightly divide the
words and from then on the Spirit really could "use"
me.

As preachers, we need to study the word for
proper preaching but we need to study it so we can
be strengthened and ministered to ourselves. We
need to study so we can overcome OUR problems and
weaknesses.

Along with studying the bible, we need to read
and study those things that will help us grow and do
better at rightly dividing the word. School is a good
way to prepare yourself. You need a little more than
just a "passion" and your calling. Would you go to a
mechanic that just had a passion and a calling but
he has failed to update himself on new cars?
Would you want to go to a doctor that only had a
passion and no information, they are still practicing
medicine the way it was done in the 1960's? There

have been a lot of new discoveries since then. There is a song that says I've got Jesus and that's enough, that may be true as far as salvation but you will need a little more to be the preacher that He wants you to be. I know that may sound blasphemous to some but HIS word says to study, His word in John 8 speaks of the benefits of *continuing* in His word.

As I said, school is a good thing, if you can go please do. You may say that you are not able to do that right now. Maybe you can go part time or you can take a class or two. If you can't do that, read some books or go to some seminars. It is essential that you do something to improve yourself as a vessel to be used by God.

Please be advised that studying, growing and getting better will not be free, it will cost you. Cost you some TIME, you have to set aside some time in your schedule to do some growth producing things. This growth will not only cost you some time but it will also cost you some MONEY. You have to be willing to spend the money on your betterment. If you get an honorarium from a preaching engagement, sometimes you can use some of it to buy a book, an instructional cd or go to a seminar. If you want to be a

workman that will not be ashamed, it is going to cost
you. You should be willing to pay the cost. No matter
how well you can sing, no matter how well you can
"hoop", no matter what you look like, nothing takes
the place of studying, because that's what we are told
to do in order to rightly divide the word of truth.
STUDY, not just pray, STUDY, not sing, STUDY, not
dress well, STUDY, STUDY!!!

In talking about rightly dividing the word, it is
important to mention that there are an innumerable
amount of tools to help you do that. Yes you need
the Holy Ghost but a book, a dictionary, a
concordance would be good also. There are many
software programs that you can get. There are helps
that you can get while you are working towards
being able to afford some of the more expensive
helps, if that is an issue. There are study bibles; a
Hebrew Greek study Bible is very helpful. Giving you
the words in the original language. This can help
you to have a better understanding of what the writer
meant when he wrote it. There are Bibles that give
information on the city that a letter may have been
written to. Many Bibles have this in the introduction
of the letter. There are even some free software

downloads that you can use, one is called e-sword. It gives definitions and other helpful information.

There will be those that say it doesn't take all of that. That depends on what you want to do. If you want to continually make straight cuts, these things will probably help. You will have those that say their grandfather and other preachers from another era didn't have all of that stuff and they were great preachers. No they didn't but just imagine, as great as they were, what would have happened if they had access to some of the helps, to join with their anointing? The reason they didn't have these things is pretty obvious, not that they did not need them or could not use them, many of them didn't exist yet.

It was mentioned that the words rightly divide are translated from words that mean to make a straight cut. To regularly make a straight cut, one would need to regularly have sharp tools.

Preparation

Regular preparation is essential. You should want to be ready when an opportunity does come along. Opportunities may come at any time. If you regularly prepare and have good preparation habits you will be ready whenever a preaching engagement does come along. I can remember when I started preaching, I did what I called "writing" a sermon every week. Now before you think I was on an ego trip, I did come to realize two things, first I was not going to be preaching anywhere that often. The second thing was, most of what I was writing was not worth preaching anyway.

What it did do for me was to prepare me for studying regularly and it gave me some good habits. When an opportunity did come along, I was ready and I had something to work with. This also helped in case a preaching assignment did come along and I didn't have a week or two prior notice. I have heard a saying by some more seasoned preachers that you should have a sermon in your head, one in your heart and one in your pocket. What that translates to is, be ye also ready. This helped me when I started pastoring and I was preaching every week.

Preparing the Message

I want to say a few words about the mechanics of sermon preparation. Along with having the right tools, it is important to have the right habits and techniques. The following are some words that the preacher that rightly divides the words should know and have a good grasp of:

Exegesis

This is a word that means to lead out from. In other words, proper exegesis is when one starts with what the text says and goes from there to give the proper explanation and not trying to find or twist a verse to fit YOUR idea.

Eisegesis

This means to put into the text. In other words when people add something to what the Bible says, they add what "they" think. For example, in John 8, dealing with the woman that was caught in adultery and Jesus stoops down to write on the ground. Some preachers have attempted to say what He wrote, to do that would be eisegesis, because there is nothing in that text to suggest what he may have written. One has to be careful of this practice. There is probably not much anointing on eisegesis, but there is likely to be on proper exegesis.

Hermeneutics

This is the process or science of interpreting what a passage of scripture means. This process enables the preacher to not only know what the verse says but what it means. For example Psalms 27:2 says

*When the wicked even, mine **enemies** and my **foes**, came upon me to eat up my flesh, they stumbled and fell.*

Proper exegeses will say start with what the text says and here it speaks of enemies and foes. Proper hermeneutics causes you to look at the fact that it

SAYS enemies and foes, which in most people's mind are the same thing. Proper interpretation may cause you to ask why use two words if they are the same thing? In this text the words mean two different things. The word *enemy* in that text is the word: tsar tsar *(tsar, tsawr)* its Hebrew definition is *-narrow*; (as a noun) a *tight* place (usually figuratively, trouble). The word *foe* in that text is from the Hebrew word: 'ôyêb 'ôyêb *(o-yabe', o-yabe') hating*; an *adversary.* So although the text says two words that, in our language mean the same thing, these two words mean two different things. One word is talking about a place or predicament and the other is talking about a type of person.

Homiletics

This is the art and science of saying the same thing that the scripture says. The previous terms we dealt with are the process of getting to the point of doing what this words means. It may be called the study or art of sermon preparation.

Exposition or Expository Preaching

All of the above components come together to bring the preacher to what is called Expository Preaching. That is to expose the text, to lay it open and say what it says and show that it means what it means.

Sermon or lesson organization

A sermon or lesson needs to be properly composed and organized. This gives the message structure and helps the people follow you. Rick Warren says that when we preach, it should be to get the people to do something. That can be difficult if they can't follow you. There are certain parts to the development or organization:

The Introduction

This sets the people up to go on the trip and it tells them where they are going. A good introduction should gain the audience's attention. This is the part where you tell them what you are going to tell them. It should introduce the text that is being preached and it should state the proposition or focus. You know what you are going to say, you have been dealing with it for a few days, the people need to know, so they can follow along. The introduction should establish relevancy, this gives the people a reason to even listen to you, to determine if they want to go where you are going. The introduction should state the expectation. The preacher is saying something and there is a desired intent for something to be done with what has been said. Jesus' sermons are filled with, in word or implication, plenty of: "go and do like wise".

The Exposition

It may also be called the body, this is the section where you tell them what you said you were going to tell them. This is the journey that was talked about in the introduction. The nature of the exposition is to present, explain and expound other ideas and information of the text. This is where you make the straight cuts.

This development involves revisiting the material that has been amplified, organizing the result of the preparation, arranging the information into different divisions and subdivisions. Some of the tools for the development of this section may include commentaries, quotations and the information attained from the study that was spoken of earlier.

The Close or Wrap up

The nature of the summation is, this is where you bring it all together and maybe tell them what you told them or recognize that you are arriving at the previously stated destination. Some may call this the conclusion but then there are those that say it is not "concluded" until the people perform the principles that have been preached .

There are certain steps to the summation, they include the recap, this is a short review of the proposition of the sermon. Illustration, a story or anecdote that highlights what you are attempting to convey. The application, a few examples of how the listener can put into practice what the preacher just told them. Quotation, this can come in the form of a standout statement that drives home the focus of the sermon. A question, a thought provoking question that will cause the listener to deal with the relevant points of the sermon. The Appeal, a plea for the listener to make this word alive in their life after the benediction. A good summation can/ should reflect the proposition; it should fit the essence of the message. It should be clear in thought and expression. If the goal of the message is to get the people to DO something, they can't do what they can't follow. (It was worth repeating)

This may not be the absolute in preparation but it will be helpful as you begin preparing organized sermons and lessons. This will help you line up with the scripture that says all things should be done decently and in order. The word translated "order" in that verse is a Greek word that means regular arrangement. When things are arranged they don't just go any and everywhere. They don't just "end up" somewhere.

Preparing the messenger

It is not only necessary to properly prepare the message but the messenger, THAT'S YOU. It is important to have good health so that you can be a good vessel. It is important that our lifestyle and behavior match the calling. This is important because you are a proclaimer of the gospel, we have a responsibility to exegete the word but also to exhibit that same word. Preaching the gospel and ministering to people is a serious task, we should not do anything to mess that up. It is important that we check our behavior. We want to be good representatives of "OUR BOSS".

Render therefore to all their dues: tribute to whom tribute is due; custom to whom custom; fear to whom fear; honour to whom honour. Rm. 13:7

Supporting Your Pastor

Let me say a word to new preachers (and the not so new) about supporting your Pastor. The Pastor is your spiritual covering. There should be some loyalty given to them. It is the vision that the Lord gave THEM that is to be put forth at the local congregation that you are a part of. We should all pray for, show love for and support our Pastors.

Never, never correct or disagree with your Pastor in public, in a way that could demonstrate division or insubordination. Does this mean that you are not to have your own mind? of course not. But if there is something that you disagree with, you should talk to them privately. They may give you some insight on the particular issue or they may see something that you don't or can't. After your conversation, if you still disagree you should still support. When I say disagree, I'm speaking basically of methodology, a ministry idea or something like that. This is not asking anyone to support something that is biblically wrong.

I even want to say something about that. I think a person should give their Pastor support right or wrong. This may sound contradictory but stay with me. I did not say support the wrong that the Pastor may do. The Pastor may do something that is biblically wrong, they still deserve some support and support means to pray for, to help in their restoration, to protect. If the Pastor has done something wrong and they are attempting to fix it, you should support that. All of us have and will make some errors, wouldn't you want someone to pray for you or give you another chance? In this you are showing respect for the position, even if you can't show it for the person.

You may be saying what if the person is not trying to change and you can't support them anymore? They are still the Pastor and if you are going to a part

60

of that congregation you are either going to be a part of the solution or a part of the problem. If you can't be a part of the solution and the Pastor is not going anywhere, maybe you should be prayerful about being a part of that congregation.

The scriptures tell us in 1Chronichles 16:22 to touch not God's anointed and to do His prophet no harm. The text does not say only when they are right. Pastors need the effectual fervent prayers of the righteous that avail much. You need to make sure that you pray for and properly support your Pastor, because you may become a Pastor some day and you may, no check that, you WILL have people that dislike and disagree with what you do and you may even make a mistake or two. You will need and want to have the support of the people that you are leading. Here are some ways that you can support your Pastor:

Support by what you say

Exodus 32 speaks of an occasion when Moses was away praying, (his prayers likely had to do with the people at the bottom of the hill) the people got tired of waiting for him and asked his brother,(associate minister, assistant to the Pastor) what has become of him. This resulted in Aaron not showing the proper support for his "Pastor" and helped the people make a golden calf and throw a party. What he SHOULD have said was that Moses was praying for them and reminded them of the other times he talked to God on their behalf.

At one point the people began to give praise to the god that they just made, giving it credit for some of their benefits. What should Aaron have said? He should have spoken to them about all that the Lord had done, bringing them through the Red Sea, helping them with water and manna. He should have reminded them that it was Moses that was the messenger of God that was used to do all of these things. He should have lifted up the Pastor (Moses) and reminded the people of what Moses was doing on their behalf. Not only did he not SAY something to support the Pastor, he initiated some of the wrong things that the people did while the "Pastor" was away, doing something FOR THEM.

Eventually Moses came back down and there were consequences. The result was that the calf that they made had to be ground up and put in some water and the people had to drink it. There are consequences for not showing support to the shepherd.

Support by what you show

And he drank of the wine, and was drunken; and he was uncovered within his tent. And Ham, the father of Canaan, saw the nakedness of his father, and told his two brethren without. And Shem and Japheth took a garment, and laid it upon both their shoulders, and went backward, and covered the nakedness of their father; and their faces were backward, and they saw not their father's nakedness. Gen.9:21-23

This text shows an account of a father and sons but the principle I want to show is support of those over you. The father was drunk, he messed up. There may be a time when your Pastor DOES make a mistake. Now I'm not referring to someone that is not trying to get better, but a person that is being human and humans DO make mistakes. Noah was drunk and his first son did not do anything to help. The wording in the text suggests that he did just the opposite. The text says that he *told his brothers.* That seems like an okay thing to do but the word, *told* in that text is nâgad-(*naw-gad'*) it means to *front*, that is, stand boldly out, opposite; by implication, to *manifest*;

figuratively to *announce* (always by word of mouth to one present); specifically to *expose, explain, praise.*

This suggests that Ham went to his brothers and made fun of their father, he talked badly about the situation, he spoke against the father, he showed disrespect. He did not do or say anything that was productive. But you say Noah WAS guilty. Ham should have, in this case supported or helped his father. You say was he supposed to make a COVER UP? no but he should have done a COVER-ING. That is what his brothers did. The text shows us that they took something and covered him and they did not even look on his nakedness. What Ham did, resulted in a curse on Canaan from his father, so there must have been something wrong with what he did.

This is one way of showing support for those over you. Another way is by praying for them. How often do you really PRAY for your Pastor, praying for his health, their family? Even for them to overcome any faults or weakness they may have. Sometimes we will talk to others about them but why not talk to God about them?

Support by what you sow

I know this can be a controversial subject; people have problems when it comes to preachers and money. It costs to do anything, so why would a person think that ministry would be any different? People do want their Pastor to come see them in the hospital, go see someone at the court house and come to do their loved one's funeral.

Most Pastors do work another job, so they have to take off, if they can, to do some of these things. If they come to the hospital they have to drive to get there, they have to pay for parking. Why would you not want them to be able to do these things? Why would you not want to help them to do those things? Not only that but you do want your Pastor to be equipped to rightly divide the word, don't you?

Helping the Pastor would also be in line with the word and will help you by being blessed. I know that sounds like a line to get you to give them money, let's look at scripture.

But my God shall supply all your need according to his riches in glory by Christ Jesus. Phil 4:19

This is a verse of scripture that many people like to quote, but they tend start at verse 19 but this is the result of those people doing their part.

What does the complete text say?

Now ye Philippians know also, that in the beginning of the gospel, when I departed from Macedonia, no church communicated with me as concerning giving and receiving, but ye only. For even in Thessalonica ye sent once and again unto my necessity. Not because I desire a gift: but I desire fruit that may abound to your account. But I have all, and abound: I am full, having received of Epaphroditus the things which were sent from you, an odour of a sweet smell, a sacrifice acceptable, well pleasing to God. Phil. 4:15-18

The word *communicate* in this text is the word koinōneō (*koy-no-neh'-o*) it does not mean to talk, it means to *share* with others (objectively or subjectively), it is also translated as distribute. Paul says these people gave, shared and distributed something to him. He goes on to tell what they gave, shared and distributed and why he is speaking this, that it will result in fruit for them. I know how this sounds, he is saying I am encouraging YOU to give ME money and it will help YOU. I know that sounds "pimpish" but get your Bibles and read it for yourself and see if that is not what it says. Paul seems to know the response of many people to this kind of thinking and he says it's ok to do because my God will supply all of your need…

You can support your Pastor financially by tithing to your church. No the tithe does not go to the Pastor. It takes care of the responsibilities of the church, isn't the Pastor one of those responsibilities? More specifically you can support financially through a love offering if your church does that or a special Pastoral offering, if your church does that. Maybe you can just bless them yourself in an informal way without making a big deal out of it. I would challenge you as a minister, to keep doing this, if you are presently doing this and to start if you are not. Start and see what the result will be. There is another reason you should do this, in addition to the fact that it is what the Bible says, in addition to the fact that it can help you, there may be a time when you will become a senior Pastor and you will see the principles demonstrated towards you.

While you are an assistant or staff minister (they are referred to differently in different churches) you should pray for the Pastor, obey (I know that is a word that is foreign to some peoples vocabulary), push their vision and not let anybody speak against them. They are the visionary of the house, they are your covering and you WILL REAP WHAT YOU SOW.

As I Come To a Close…

A preacher should KNOW that they are called by God. Preaching is not something you start because you think it's a good idea. If you can start because you want to preach, you can easily stop because you don't want to.

Following directions is something that should become habitual; it will help in the furthering of your ministry. We as preachers are servants   and so we should have the heart and mind of a servant.

A proper response to preaching assignments should be something that you should develop, this will avoid confusion and the Bible says that God is not the author of it, so guess who is?

Learn to invest in your ministry. Have good attire when you go preaching. That is going to vary based on the type of event where you are preaching and the particular congregation that you may be preaching for. It's good to know something about them so that you can be proper for "that" house.

Be quick to hear and slow to speak. You can benefit from being a good listener, even if what the person is saying seems to be a little off, from, it you may learn what *not* to do and who *not* to listen to in the future. Preaching styles will vary so you should just be yourself, your own style will develop as you grow.

Proper study and preparation is a must. Letting the Spirit lead you does not mean you don't study the text or not do your homework . Letting the Spirit use you is in addition to all of this, not instead of it.

Learn how to prepare a sermon or lesson. Organize it well so that people can follow what is being said. The object is to have them DO something with what you have said, which they can't do, if they can't follow what you have said.

Proper sermon preparation is important and

proper vessel preparation is equally as important. Your behavior needs to be what it should be so that you will represent *your boss* well. It may make you feel better to say that people should not be watching me, they should keep their eyes on Jesus, that is true but you and I are the representatives for Jesus. They will need to hear a thorough word so they can better see Jesus and we have to be careful not to put any road blocks in their way.

People will need to hear THE WORD, not our word because we can't do anything without it. Obviously people can't be saved without it:

For the preaching of the cross is to them that perish foolishness; but unto us which are saved it is the power of God. For it is written, I will destroy the wisdom of the wise, and will bring to nothing the understanding of the prudent. Where is the wise? where is the scribe? where is the disputer of this world? hath not God made foolish the wisdom of this world? For after that in the wisdom of God the world by wisdom knew not God, it pleased God by the foolishness of preaching to save them that believe. 1 Cor.1: 18-21

Nobody can grow without it:

> *Wherefore laying aside all malice, and all guile and hypocrisies and envies, all evil speakings. As newborn babes, desire the sincere milk of the word, that ye may grow thereby.1 Peter 2:1-2*

We can't be disciples or be free without it:

> *Then said Jesus to those Jews which believed on him, If ye continue in my word, then are ye my disciples indeed, And ye shall know the truth, and the truth shall make you free-John 8:31-32*

We will not be armed for battle without it:

> *And take the helmet of salvation, and the sword of the Spirit, which is the word of God-Ephesians 6:17*

We need to preach the word, preach the word, PREACH THE WORD!!

These pages may not cover everything that a preacher will need to know. It does however contain some things that have been helpful for me for over 30 years and I believe they can help you.

There may be some information here that you have not heard before, I hope it informs you. There may be some that you have heard before, I hope it encourages you. I hope that you use this information to assist you in becoming the preacher/minister that the Lord intends for you to be. May the Lord grow, guide and give you great blessings is my prayer.

Notes & Thoughts